Sacred Parenting: A Month of Spiritual Wisdom for Parents

By Dr. Lashawn Farrar

Sacred Parenting

Copyright Page

Sacred Parenting
A Month of Spiritual Wisdom for Parents

Copyright © 2024 by Dr. Lashawn Farrar

All rights reserved. No part of this book may be reproduced, stored in a retrieval system, or transmitted in any form or by any means, electronic, mechanical, photocopying, recording, or otherwise, without the prior written permission of the copyright owner.

For permissions, contact:
Dr. Lashawn Farrar
Email: wivesnetwork@gmail.com

Published by:
Stork Publishing LLC
700 South Boulevard Drive
Bainbridge, Georgia
Phone: 334-232-9281
Website: www.lashawndashiree.info

Publisher: Dr. Lashawnda Love

Sacred Parenting

Table of Contents

Introduction 5
Why This Book is Needed 7
Foreword 12
Day 1: Setting the Foundation 13
Day 2: Practicing Patience 15
Day 3: Cultivating Kindness 18
Day 4: Fostering Respect 21
Day 5: Encouraging Gratitude 23
Day 6: Instilling Discipline 25
Day 7: Embracing Forgiveness 28
Day 8: Nurturing Confidence 30
Day 9: Teaching Responsibility 32
Day 10: Promoting Humility 34
Day 11: Encouraging Empathy 36
Day 12: Building Trust 38
Day 13: Encouraging Perseverance 41
Day 14: Promoting Healthy Relationships ... 43
Day 15: Guiding in Decision-Making 46
Day 16: Teaching Contentment 48

Sacred Parenting

Day 17: Promoting Teamwork 50
Day 18: Fostering Creativity 52
Day 19: Encouraging Self-Reflection 55
Day 20: Teaching Servanthood 58
Day 21: Encouraging Time Management 60
Day 22: Fostering Courage 63
Day 23: Promoting Healthy Conflict Resolution . 66
Day 24: Encouraging Environmental Responsibility 69
Day 25: Guiding in Healthy Eating 72
Day 26: Encouraging Lifelong Learning 75
Day 27: Teaching Humor and Joy 78
Day 28: Promoting Resourcefulness 81
Day 29: Cultivating Mindfulness 84
Day 30: Reflecting on God's Plan 87
Conclusion 90

Sacred Parenting

Introduction

The journey of parenting is a sacred odyssey, marked by profound challenges and immeasurable joys. Parents are entrusted with the pivotal task of shaping the future through the lives of their children. In the ever-evolving tapestry of the world, where change is constant and complexities abound, the timeless wisdom embedded in the pages of the Bible serves as an unwavering beacon. This devotional, ""Sacred Parenting" embarks on a transformative exploration of this divine wisdom. Its purpose is to illuminate the path of parenting with the eternal light of the Scriptures, providing parents with the unwavering guidance and fortitude necessary to raise children who

Sacred Parenting

embody compassion, confidence, and spiritual grounding.

This 30-day devotional is a heartfelt exploration of the divine guidance provided by the Bible for the intricate art of parenting. It delves into the multifaceted dimensions of parenthood, revealing profound insights and practical lessons that empower parents to cultivate children who are not only successful in the world but also deeply connected to their spiritual essence.

Why This Book is Needed

In our fast-paced digital age, parenting has taken on a new dimension, presenting challenges that previous generations never had to contend with. The advent of technology has ushered in an unprecedented influx of information, simultaneously a boon and a burden. Parents find themselves bombarded with conflicting advice, societal pressures, and the constant demands of modern life. Amidst this cacophony, the task of parenting has become not only daunting but also overwhelming.

The virtual realm, with its social media platforms and instant connectivity, exposes children and parents alike to a barrage of influences, not all of which are positive. The pressure to measure up to societal standards and navigate the complexities of online interactions adds layers of stress to an already challenging role. In this era, where the line between the real and the virtual blurs, parents grapple with unique dilemmas, from screen time battles to addressing cyberbullying.

Moreover, the pace of life in the 21st century is relentless. Parents juggle demanding careers, social obligations, and familial responsibilities, often finding little time for self-reflection or recharging their own spiritual batteries. The result is a generation of parents feeling adrift, seeking solid ground amidst the whirlwind of modern existence.

This book is crafted to address these challenges.

"Nurturing Souls: A 30-Day Parenting Devotional Guided by Biblical Wisdom" is more than a mere guide; it is a lifeline for parents navigating the stormy seas of contemporary parenting. Rooted in faith and infused with the timeless wisdom of the

Bible, this book serves as a sanctuary of calm amidst the chaos.

Practical Solutions in a Faithful Context: This devotional doesn't just acknowledge the challenges; it provides practical, real-world solutions grounded in faith. It offers tangible strategies to manage screen time, foster open communication, and build resilience in children. These solutions are not arbitrary; they are firmly rooted in the deep well of biblical teachings, providing parents with a rock-solid foundation upon which to base their decisions.

A Source of Reassurance and Strength: In the pages of this book, parents will find reassurance. It whispers the ageless truths of the scriptures, reminding them that they are not alone in their struggles. Each daily reading offers a moment of reflection, a chance to pause amidst the frenzy and reconnect with a source of divine strength. It reminds parents that the challenges they face are not insurmountable, for they are guided by a faith that has withstood the test of time.

Empowering Parents for Today and Tomorrow: Beyond immediate challenges, this book equips parents with tools that have enduring relevance. By delving into the timeless principles of love, patience, compassion, and resilience found in the Bible, parents are not just addressing the issues of today; they are nurturing the foundations of character that will serve their children well into the future.

In a world that constantly bombards parents with noise, "Nurturing Souls" stands as a beacon of quiet wisdom. It's a reminder that amidst the whirlwind of modernity, the ancient truths of love, faith, and family are not only relevant but also more crucial than ever. This book offers parents a steadfast

Sacred Parenting

anchor, helping them not only weather the storms of the present but also navigate the uncharted waters of the future with grace, faith, and unwavering strength.

Foreword

Dear Parents,

In the journey of parenting, we often find ourselves seeking guidance, reassurance, and inspiration. This 30-day guide is more than just a collection of advice; it's a companion designed to walk with you through the joys and challenges of raising your child. Rooted in the wisdom of the Bible, each day offers insights, practical tips, and reflections to empower you in your role as a parent.

Remember, you are not alone on this journey. As you delve into the pages of this guide, may you find the strength to parent with purpose, the wisdom to make thoughtful decisions, and the grace to nurture the unique spirit of your child.

Sacred Parenting

Blessings,

Day 1: Setting the Foundation

Scripture: Proverbs 22:6 (KJV)

"Train up a child in the way he should go: and when he is old, he will not depart from it."

Word or Phrase: Foundation in Faith

Declaration: Today, I declare my commitment to building a foundation in faith for my child. I acknowledge the profound impact of nurturing their spirit and guiding them on a path rooted in love and trust in the divine.

Motivation: As parents, we are entrusted with the sacred duty of shaping young minds and spirits. By grounding our parenting in faith, we offer our children an unshakable foundation upon which they can build their lives. Just as a solid foundation supports a towering structure, our faith will support our children through life's challenges and triumphs.

Reflection: Reflect upon your own faith journey. Consider the moments when your faith provided comfort and strength. Imagine imparting this same enduring faith to your child, ensuring that they have a source of unwavering support in their lives.

Prayer: Dear Heavenly Father, on this first day of our parenting journey, we come before you with hearts filled with gratitude and hope. We commit ourselves to raising our child in the light of your love, teaching them the ways of faith, compassion, and grace. May our home be a sanctuary of faith, and may our child's heart be receptive to your teachings. Grant us the wisdom to be steadfast guides, leading our little one on a path of righteousness. In your holy name, we pray. Amen.

Sacred Parenting

Day 2: Practicing Patience

Scripture

James 1:19 (KJV) - Wherefore, my beloved brethren, let every man be swift to hear, slow to speak, slow to wrath:

Declaration

Today, I declare that I will cultivate the virtue of patience in my interactions with others, especially with my children. I will strive to be swift to listen, slow to speak, and slow to anger, embodying the patience that God bestows upon me.

Motivation

In our fast-paced world, patience is a rare treasure. It allows us to understand deeply, to respond thoughtfully, and to foster connections that stand the test of time. As parents, our patience becomes a guiding light for our children, teaching them the art of understanding, empathy, and resilience.

Reflection

Patience is not merely the ability to wait but the power to keep a good attitude while waiting. In the moments of frustration, I will remember the wisdom of James 1:19. I will recall that being slow to anger doesn't signify weakness; rather, it showcases the strength of self-control and the depth of understanding.

In every challenging situation, I will breathe, pause, and listen. I will seek to comprehend not only the words spoken but also the emotions underlying them. By practicing patience, I sow the seeds of harmony, grace, and love within my family.

Prayer

Sacred Parenting

Dear Lord, Grant me the patience to listen attentively, the wisdom to respond with kindness, and the strength to remain calm in challenging situations. Help me emulate your divine patience in my interactions with my children, teaching them the beauty of understanding and the power of self-restraint. May my actions reflect your love, and may my patience be a testament to the peace that resides within me.

In your patient and loving name, I pray.

Amen.

Day 3: Cultivating Kindness

Scripture: *Ephesians 4:32 (KJV) - And be ye kind one to another, tenderhearted, forgiving one another, even as God for Christ's sake hath forgiven you.*

Declaration: Today, I declare that kindness will be the language of my heart. I choose to embrace kindness not just as a gesture but as a way of being. I will teach my child the profound importance of empathy, understanding, and forgiveness in their interactions with others.

Motivation: Kindness is a universal language that transcends boundaries and heals wounds. It's more than mere politeness; it's a transformative force that can mend broken relationships, bring comfort to the weary, and instill hope in the hopeless. As I cultivate kindness in my child, I'm sowing the seeds of a compassionate world.

Reflection: Ephesians 4:32 reminds us of God's boundless kindness and forgiveness toward us. In the face of our shortcomings, He showers us with love and understanding. As parents, we are tasked with mirroring this divine kindness in our daily lives, becoming living examples for our children.

Today, I reflect on the times when a small act of kindness from someone else made a significant impact on my day. It may have been a smile, a kind word, or a thoughtful gesture. I ponder on how such moments have the power to change lives, including my own.

Prayer: Dear Lord,

Help me and my child embrace kindness as a way of life. Let our hearts be tender, our words be gentle, and our actions be compassionate. Teach us the art of forgiveness, reminding us that we are all

Sacred Parenting

flawed and in need of grace. May our lives be a testament to your boundless love, reflecting kindness to everyone we encounter.

In your loving and kind name, I pray.

Amen.

Day 4: Fostering Respect

Scripture: *1 Peter 2:17 (KJV) - Honour all men. Love the brotherhood. Fear God. Honour the king.*

Declaration: Today, I declare my commitment to fostering respect in my child's heart. I choose to honor all individuals, recognizing the inherent value in each soul. I will teach my child the importance of treating everyone with dignity, for in respect, we find the bridge to understanding and harmony.

Motivation: Respect is the cornerstone of harmonious relationships. It transcends differences, creating a space where empathy and understanding can thrive. As I instill this virtue in my child, I am shaping not just their character but also the world they inhabit. Through respect, we sow the seeds of a compassionate and united society.

Reflection: 1 Peter 2:17 offers profound wisdom: honoring all, loving our brethren, fearing God, and respecting authority. Today, I reflect on the times when I felt truly respected by others and how it uplifted my spirit. I contemplate the transformative power of respect in resolving conflicts and building bridges between diverse perspectives.

Prayer: Dear Lord,

Grant me the wisdom to teach my child the essence of respect. Help us honor every individual, recognizing the divine spark within them. Guide us to treat others with kindness, dignity, and understanding, irrespective of our differences. May our actions reflect the reverence we have for You, O Lord, in how we respect and honor others.

In Your holy name, I pray. Amen.

Day 5: Encouraging Gratitude

Scripture: *1 Thessalonians 5:18 (KJV) - In everything give thanks: for this is the will of God in Christ Jesus concerning you.*

Declaration: Today, I declare that gratitude will be the melody of our family. In every moment, I choose to give thanks. I will encourage my child to appreciate the blessings in their life, fostering a heart overflowing with thankfulness.

Motivation: Gratitude is the gateway to joy and contentment. It transforms our perception, enabling us to see beauty in the ordinary and blessings in every circumstance. As I nurture gratitude in my child, I am planting the seeds of a positive outlook, resilience, and a heart attuned to the abundant goodness of life.

Sacred Parenting

Reflection: 1 Thessalonians 5:18 reminds us to give thanks in everything. Today, I reflect on the moments when gratitude lifted my spirit, bringing peace amidst chaos. I contemplate the power of a simple 'thank you' and its ability to strengthen relationships. Gratitude, I realize, is a bridge connecting us to God's abundant grace.

Prayer: Dear Lord,

Open our hearts to the beauty of gratitude. Teach us to appreciate not just the grand blessings but also the small miracles of everyday life. Help us instill in our child a heart brimming with thankfulness, for in gratitude, we find contentment and in thanksgiving, we discover joy. May our family be a testament to Your abundant grace.

In Your name, we pray.

Amen.

Day 6: Instilling Discipline

Scripture: *Proverbs 13:24 (KJV) - He that spareth his rod hateth his son: but he that loveth him chasteneth him betimes.*

Declaration: Today, I declare my commitment to nurturing my child with love and discipline in balance. I understand that boundaries and consequences are essential for their growth. I will teach my child the importance of responsibility, accountability, and the enduring power of love.

Motivation: Discipline, when rooted in love, becomes a guiding light for children. It provides them with a sense of structure, security, and a foundation upon which they can build their character. By teaching discipline, I am helping my child navigate life's challenges with resilience and integrity.

Reflection: Proverbs 13:24 offers profound insight into the delicate balance between love and discipline. Today, I reflect on moments when discipline was an act of love, guiding me or someone I know toward a better path. I contemplate the wisdom in setting boundaries, understanding consequences, and the transformative power of disciplined choices.

Prayer: Dear Lord,

Grant me the wisdom to discipline my child with love. Help me set boundaries that nurture their spirit and consequences that teach responsibility. May my discipline always be rooted in love, guiding them toward the right path with kindness and understanding. Strengthen our bond through these lessons, and may they grow into responsible, compassionate adults.

In Your name, I pray.

Amen.

Day 7: Embracing Forgiveness

Scripture: *Colossians 3:13 (KJV) - Forbearing one another, and forgiving one another, if any man have a quarrel against any: even as Christ forgave you, so also do ye.*

Declaration: Today, I declare that forgiveness will be the cornerstone of our family. I choose to embrace the healing power of letting go and reconciling with love. I will teach my child the art of forgiveness, guiding them toward a heart free from grudges and a spirit open to reconciliation.

Motivation: Forgiveness is not just a gift we give to others; it's a gift we give to ourselves. It liberates us from the burdens of anger and resentment, fostering inner peace and harmony. As I explore forgiveness, I am teaching my child the profound strength found in letting go and the transformative power of reconciliation.

Reflection: Colossians 3:13 urges us to forgive as Christ forgave us. Today, I reflect on moments of forgiveness in my life, recalling the peace that followed. I contemplate the grace inherent in forgiving others, recognizing that in letting go, we create space for love and understanding to flourish.

Prayer: Dear Lord,

Grant us the strength to forgive as you forgave us. Help us embrace the healing power of letting go, understanding that forgiveness does not condone actions but liberates our souls. Guide me in teaching my child the art of forgiveness, that they may carry a heart unburdened by grudges and filled with love.

In Your name, I pray.

Amen.

Day 8: Nurturing Confidence

Scripture: *Philippians 4:13 (KJV) - I can do all things through Christ which strengtheneth me.*

Declaration: Today, I declare that I will nurture confidence in my child. I will remind them daily of their inherent strength, teaching them that with faith, they can overcome any challenge. I will empower them to believe in themselves, for through Christ, they are capable of achieving great things.

Motivation: Confidence is the cornerstone of courage and achievement. By nurturing confidence in my child, I am giving them the wings to soar, to dream, and to believe in their abilities. In the light of their faith, they can face any obstacle with unwavering determination.

Sacred Parenting

Reflection: Philippians 4:13 reminds us of the boundless strength we receive through Christ. Today, I reflect on the moments when my faith propelled me forward, giving me the courage to tackle the seemingly insurmountable. I contemplate the transformative power of self-belief and the impact it can have on shaping a resilient and confident spirit.

Prayer: Dear Lord,

Grant my child the gift of unwavering confidence. Help them understand that their abilities are a divine blessing, and with faith in You, they can conquer any challenge. Strengthen their spirit, Lord, and let them walk with the knowledge that they are capable, resilient, and deeply loved. May their confidence be a testament to Your grace.

In Jesus' name, I pray.

Amen.

Day 9: Teaching Responsibility

Scripture: *Galatians 6:5 (KJV) - For every man shall bear his own burden.*

Declaration: Today, I declare my commitment to teaching my child responsibility. I will guide them to understand the importance of accountability and taking ownership of their actions. I will empower them to be responsible individuals, recognizing that their choices shape their destiny.

Motivation: Responsibility is the cornerstone of maturity and self-reliance. By teaching my child to bear their own burdens, I am preparing them for the challenges of life. I am nurturing resilience and a strong work ethic, enabling them to face the future with confidence and determination.

Reflection: Galatians 6:5 reminds us of the individual responsibility we bear. Today, I reflect on the times when taking responsibility for my actions led to growth and self-discovery. I contemplate the transformative power of accountability and the strength it provides in facing life's trials.

Prayer: Dear Lord,

Grant my child the wisdom to understand the importance of responsibility. Help them recognize that their actions shape their future. Guide me in teaching them the value of accountability and ownership. May they grow into responsible individuals, strong in character and steadfast in their commitments.

In Your name, I pray.

Amen.

Day 10: Promoting Humility

Scripture: *Philippians 2:3 (KJV) - Let nothing be done through strife or vainglory; but in lowliness of mind let each esteem other better than themselves.*

Declaration: Today, I declare my dedication to promoting humility in my child. I will guide them to understand that true strength lies in serving others, considering their needs above their own. I will nurture in them a spirit of selflessness and kindness, for in humility, they find grace and harmony.

Motivation: Humility is the foundation of genuine compassion. By promoting humility, I am nurturing a heart that beats in harmony with the needs of others. It is through acts of service and considering others as valuable that we truly understand the depth of the human spirit.

Reflection: Philippians 2:3 reminds us of the profound beauty in esteeming others higher than ourselves. Today, I reflect on moments when I practiced humility and the peace it brought into my life. I contemplate the transformative power of selfless acts and the impact they have on building meaningful connections with others.

Prayer: Dear Lord,

Instill in my child the virtue of humility. Teach them to serve others with a heart full of love and kindness. Guide me in nurturing their spirit to consider the needs of others before their own. May they find joy in selflessness and strength in humility, understanding that in serving others, they serve You.

In Your name, I pray.

Amen.

Day 11: Encouraging Empathy

Scripture: *Romans 12:15 (KJV) - Rejoice with them that do rejoice, and weep with them that weep.*

Declaration: Today, I declare my commitment to encouraging empathy in my child. I will guide them to understand the feelings of others, rejoicing in their joys and comforting them in their sorrows. I will nurture in them a compassionate heart, for in empathy, they find the true essence of humanity.

Motivation: Empathy is the cornerstone of compassion. By encouraging empathy, I am nurturing a spirit that connects deeply with the joys and sorrows of others. It allows us to celebrate with the triumphant and console the grieving, creating bonds that transcend words and actions.

Reflection: Romans 12:15 reminds us to share in the emotions of others. Today, I reflect on the times when someone's empathy touched my soul, bringing comfort in moments of despair and multiplying the joy in moments of triumph. I contemplate the transformative power of empathy and the healing it brings to the human spirit.

Prayer: Dear Lord,

Grant my child the gift of empathy. Help them understand the emotions of others, rejoicing in their happiness and comforting them in their pain. Guide me in nurturing their spirit to connect deeply with the feelings of those around them. May they grow into compassionate individuals, spreading the light of understanding and love wherever they go.

In Your name, I pray.

Amen.

Day 12: Building Trust

Scripture: *Proverbs 3:5-6 (KJV) - Trust in the Lord with all thine heart; and lean not unto thine own understanding. In all thy ways acknowledge him, and he shall direct thy paths.*

Declaration: Today, I declare my dedication to teaching my child the profound importance of trust. I will guide them to trust in relationships, both with others and with You, dear Lord. I emphasize faith and reliance on Your divine guidance, understanding that in trust, we find the foundation for strong, lasting connections.

Motivation: Trust is the cornerstone of deep, meaningful relationships. By teaching my child the importance of trusting others and surrendering to Your divine wisdom, I am nurturing their spirit to navigate life's complexities with faith. In trust, we find the courage to let go and the strength to move forward.

Reflection: Proverbs 3:5-6 reminds us to trust in the Lord with all our hearts. Today, I reflect on the times when I placed my trust in You, dear Lord, and how You directed my paths with grace and wisdom. I contemplate the transformative power of trust in human relationships, recognizing that it forms the bedrock of love and understanding.

Prayer: Dear Lord,

Grant my child the gift of unwavering trust. Help them trust in You with all their heart, understanding that Your guidance is the true north in their lives. Teach them to trust others wisely, and may their relationships be built on a foundation of faith. May they find the strength and courage that come from

Sacred Parenting

trust, and may their trust in You deepen their connection with You and with others.

In Your holy name, I pray. Amen.

Day 13: Encouraging Perseverance

Scripture: *Galatians 6:9 (KJV) - And let us not be weary in well doing: for in due season we shall reap, if we faint not.*

Declaration: Today, I declare my commitment to nurturing perseverance in my child. I will inspire them to face challenges with unwavering determination, reminding them of the rewards that come to those who persist. I will instill in them the belief that in perseverance, they find the strength to overcome obstacles and the courage to triumph against all odds.

Motivation: Perseverance is the key that unlocks the doors of achievement. By encouraging my child to persist in their endeavors, I am empowering them to transform setbacks into stepping stones. In the face of adversity, perseverance fuels hope and fuels the drive to succeed.

Reflection: Galatians 6:9 reminds us not to grow weary in well-doing. Today, I reflect on the times when I persevered through challenges and emerged stronger. I contemplate the transformative power of determination, understanding that every trial we face is an opportunity for growth.

Prayer: Dear Lord,

Grant my child the gift of unwavering perseverance. May they find strength in the face of challenges and determination in times of difficulty. Help them see obstacles as opportunities and setbacks as setups for comebacks. In their perseverance, may they discover the depth of their own resilience and the boundless possibilities that lie ahead.

In Your name, I pray.

Amen.

Day 14: Promoting Healthy Relationships

Scripture: *1 Corinthians 13:4-5 (KJV) - Charity suffereth long, and is kind; charity envieth not; charity vaunteth not itself, is not puffed up, Doth not behave itself unseemly, seeketh not her own, is not easily provoked, thinketh no evil;*

Declaration: Today, I declare my commitment to promoting healthy and nurturing relationships in my child's life. I will explore the profound qualities of love as described in Corinthians, teaching my child to be patient, kind, humble, and understanding. I will guide them to seek genuine connections, where love and respect form the

Sacred Parenting

foundation, fostering relationships that enrich their spirit and the lives of others.

Motivation: Love, as described in Corinthians, serves as the blueprint for healthy relationships. By instilling these qualities in my child, I am empowering them to build relationships that are enduring and uplifting. In cultivating love, we sow the seeds of understanding, empathy, and a harmonious coexistence with others.

Reflection: 1 Corinthians 13:4-5 outlines the characteristics of love. Today, I reflect on these qualities and how they manifest in my own relationships. I contemplate the transformative power of love, recognizing that it has the ability to heal wounds, bridge gaps, and create bonds that withstand the test of time.

Prayer: Dear Lord, Guide my child to understand the depth of love described in Corinthians. Help them embody the qualities of patience, kindness, humility, and understanding in their relationships.

Sacred Parenting

May they seek connections based on genuine love and respect, and may their interactions with others be a source of joy and fulfillment. Bless them with the wisdom to nurture healthy relationships that reflect the love and compassion You have for us.

In Your loving name, I pray. Amen.

Day 15: Guiding in Decision-Making

Scripture: *Psalm 32:8 (KJV) - I will instruct thee and teach thee in the way which thou shalt go: I will guide thee with mine eye.*

Declaration: Today, I declare my commitment to seeking God's guidance in decision-making. I will teach my child the importance of prayer and divine direction in their choices. I believe that God instructs us and guides us with His loving eye, illuminating our path and leading us toward decisions that align with His divine purpose.

Motivation: In a world filled with choices and complexities, seeking God's guidance provides us with clarity and peace. By teaching my child to turn to God in prayer, I am empowering them to make decisions rooted in faith. Divine direction ensures that their choices are aligned with God's plan, leading them toward a purposeful and fulfilling life.

Reflection: Psalm 32:8 reassures us of God's promise to guide us. Today, I reflect on moments when I sought God's guidance and witnessed the blessings that followed. I contemplate the transformative power of divine direction, understanding that in God's light, we find the way forward.

Prayer: Dear Lord,

I come before You seeking Your divine guidance in every decision I make. Illuminate my path with Your wisdom and lead me with Your loving eye. Help me teach my child the importance of prayer and faith in decision-making. May they always seek Your direction and find confidence in the choices guided by Your divine hand. In Your presence, I find assurance and peace.

In Your holy name, I pray. Amen.

Day 16: Teaching Contentment

Scripture: *Philippians 4:11 (KJV) - Not that I speak in respect of want: for I have learned, in whatsoever state I am, therewith to be content.*

Declaration: Today, I declare my commitment to teaching my child the profound virtue of contentment. I will guide them to appreciate what they have, finding joy in simplicity, and embracing gratitude for life's blessings. I believe that true contentment is found in a heart filled with gratitude and a spirit that finds joy in every moment.

Motivation: In a world that constantly craves more, teaching contentment becomes an invaluable lesson. By cultivating a spirit of gratitude, my child will learn to appreciate the abundance in simplicity. Contentment fosters a sense of peace and fulfillment, allowing us to find joy in the present moment and appreciate the beauty of life's little blessings.

Reflection: Philippians 4:11 speaks of contentment regardless of circumstances. Today, I reflect on moments of pure contentment in my own life, recognizing that these moments were not defined by possessions but by the joy of being alive. I contemplate the transformative power of appreciating what we have, understanding that in gratitude, we find true wealth.

Prayer: Dear Lord, Grant my child the wisdom to find contentment in simplicity. Teach them the beauty of gratitude, and help them appreciate the richness of life's blessings, both big and small. May their heart be a sanctuary of contentment, finding joy in every moment and appreciating the

Sacred Parenting

abundance of Your love. In a world of wants, guide them to find peace in what they have.

In Your name, I pray. Amen.

Day 17: Promoting Teamwork

Scripture: *Ecclesiastes 4:9-10 (KJV) - Two are better than one; because they have a good reward for their labour. For if they fall, the one will lift up his fellow: but woe to him that is alone when he falleth; for he hath not another to help him up.*

Declaration: Today, I declare my dedication to promoting the value of teamwork in my child's life. I will emphasize the strength found in unity and cooperation. Together, we can achieve more, and in helping one another, we find the true essence of humanity.

Motivation: In a world that often emphasizes individual success, teaching the importance of teamwork becomes vital. By understanding the power of collaboration, my child will learn empathy, communication, and the beauty of shared victories. Teamwork nurtures bonds and fosters a spirit of camaraderie, helping us face challenges with collective strength.

Reflection: Ecclesiastes 4:9-10 reminds us of the mutual support found in teamwork. Today, I reflect on instances where cooperation and unity led to significant accomplishments. I contemplate the transformative power of collaboration, understanding that in working together, we uplift not only ourselves but everyone around us.

Prayer: Dear Lord, bless my child with a heart that appreciates the strength of teamwork. Guide them to understand that in unity, there is immense power. Teach them the importance of cooperation, empathy, and shared success. May they find joy in lifting others and be humble in accepting help when needed. In promoting teamwork, may their life be a testament to the beauty of shared victories.

In Your name, I pray. Amen.

Day 18: Fostering Creativity

Scripture: *Genesis 1:27 (KJV) - So God created man in his own image, in the image of God created he him; male and female created he them.*

Declaration: Today, I declare my commitment to fostering creativity in my child. I will celebrate their artistic and imaginative endeavors as a reflection of God's image within them. I believe that creativity is a divine gift, and by nurturing it, I am honoring the unique and creative spirit God has instilled in my child.

Motivation: In Genesis, we are reminded that we are made in the image of God, the ultimate Creator. By fostering creativity in my child, I am

Sacred Parenting

encouraging them to explore the depths of their imagination, express their unique perspectives, and participate in the act of creation. Creativity enriches the soul, allowing us to connect with the divine spark within us.

Reflection: Genesis 1:27 emphasizes that we are created in God's image. Today, I reflect on the various forms of creativity around me – in nature, art, music, and human innovations. I contemplate the transformative power of creativity, understanding that it has the ability to inspire, heal, and bring beauty into the world.

Prayer: Dear Lord,

Thank You for gifting my child with creativity, a reflection of Your divine image within them. Guide me in nurturing their artistic and imaginative endeavors. May their creative expressions be a source of joy and fulfillment, and may they use their talents to inspire others and glorify Your name.

Sacred Parenting

Bless their creative spirit, Lord, and may it always shine brightly.

In Your creative and loving name, I pray.

Amen.

Day 19: Encouraging Self-Reflection

Scripture: *Psalm 139:23-24 (KJV) - Search me, O God, and know my heart: try me, and know my thoughts: And see if there be any wicked way in me, and lead me in the way everlasting.*

Declaration: Today, I declare my commitment to encouraging self-reflection in my child. I will guide them to seek God's guidance in understanding themselves better. I believe that self-reflection, coupled with divine wisdom, leads to personal growth, spiritual enlightenment, and a deeper connection with God.

Motivation: Self-reflection is a journey inward, a path toward self-discovery and spiritual growth. By encouraging my child to examine their thoughts, emotions, and actions, I am empowering them to align their lives with God's purpose. It fosters humility, self-awareness, and a genuine desire for transformation.

Reflection: Psalm 139:23-24 is a heartfelt plea for God to search the depths of our hearts. Today, I reflect on moments of self-reflection in my own life, acknowledging the transformative power it had. I contemplate the courage it takes to face one's true self and the grace that follows when we allow God to guide us in the process.

Prayer: Dear Lord,

Grant my child the courage to embark on the journey of self-reflection. Help them examine their thoughts, emotions, and actions with honesty and humility. May they seek Your guidance in this process, understanding that self-reflection, when coupled with Your wisdom, leads to growth and spiritual enlightenment. Guide them, Lord, and may

Sacred Parenting

Sacred Parenting

their self-discovery be a testament to Your grace and transformative power.

In Your name, I pray.

Amen.

Day 20: Teaching Servanthood

Scripture: *Mark 10:45 (KJV) - For even the Son of man came not to be ministered unto, but to minister, and to give his life a ransom for many.*

Declaration: Today, I declare my dedication to teaching my child the profound essence of servanthood. I will encourage in them a servant's heart, nurturing the fulfillment found in serving others with love and humility. I believe that true greatness is measured not by how much we receive but by how much we give.

Motivation: In Mark 10:45, Jesus exemplifies the ultimate act of servanthood. By teaching my child to serve others, I am nurturing qualities of compassion, empathy, and kindness. A servant's heart transforms lives, bringing light into the darkest corners and bridging the gaps between us. In serving others, we find purpose and fulfillment.

Reflection: Mark 10:45 reminds us of Jesus' selfless service. Today, I reflect on moments when serving others brought immense joy and fulfillment into my life. I contemplate the transformative power of humility and love, understanding that in acts of service, we reflect the divine love within us.

Prayer: Dear Lord,

Instill in my child a servant's heart. Help them understand the joy found in selfless service. May they serve others with love and humility, reflecting Your light into the world. Guide me in nurturing their compassionate spirit, and may their acts of kindness be a testament to Your love and grace. Bless them, Lord, as they become vessels of Your love through their service to others.

In Your name, I pray.

Amen.

Day 21: Encouraging Time Management

Scripture: *Ephesians 5:15-16 (KJV) - See then that ye walk circumspectly, not as fools, but as wise, Redeeming the time, because the days are evil.*

Declaration: Today, I declare my commitment to encouraging effective time management in my child. I will guide them to understand the preciousness of time and the need to use it wisely and purposefully. I believe that time is a divine gift, and managing it wisely reflects our gratitude for this gift.

Sacred Parenting

Motivation: In a world filled with distractions, teaching time management becomes vital. By emphasizing the value of each moment, my child will learn the importance of setting priorities, being organized, and making deliberate choices. Time management enhances productivity, reduces stress, and allows us to focus on what truly matters in life.

Reflection: Ephesians 5:15-16 urges us to walk wisely and redeem the time. Today, I reflect on how effectively managing my time has positively impacted my life. I contemplate the transformative power of purposeful living, understanding that by managing our time wisely, we can fulfill our responsibilities, pursue our passions, and nurture meaningful relationships.

Prayer: Dear Lord, Grant my child the wisdom to manage their time effectively. Help them discern between what is urgent and what is important. Guide me in teaching them the value of using time wisely and purposefully. May they learn to appreciate the gift of time and use it to glorify You.

Sacred Parenting

Bless their efforts, Lord, and may their days be filled with purpose and fulfillment.

In Your name, I pray.

Amen.

Day 22: Fostering Courage

Scripture: *Joshua 1:9 (KJV) - Have not I commanded thee? Be strong and of a good courage; be not afraid, neither be thou dismayed: for the Lord thy God is with thee whithersoever thou goest.*

Declaration: Today, I declare my dedication to fostering courage in my child. I will inspire them to be strong and of good courage, reminding them of God's ever-present strength in the face of challenges. I believe that courage is not the absence of fear but the triumph over it, and with God by our side, we can face any obstacle with unwavering faith.

Motivation: In Joshua 1:9, God commands us to be courageous, assuring us of His presence

Sacred Parenting

wherever we go. By instilling courage in my child, I am nurturing resilience, determination, and faith. Courage allows us to step into the unknown, confront fears, and embrace challenges with a heart fortified by God's promises.

Reflection: Joshua 1:9 reminds us of God's command to be courageous. Today, I reflect on moments in my life when courage guided my steps, leading me through trials and strengthening my faith. I contemplate the transformative power of courage, understanding that it empowers us to overcome adversity and live boldly in the light of God's love.

Prayer: Dear Lord, Instill in my child a courageous spirit. Help them face challenges with unwavering faith, knowing that You are with them wherever they go. May their courage be a testament to Your strength within them. Guide me in nurturing their bravery, and may they find confidence in Your promises. In moments of fear,

Sacred Parenting

may they find comfort in Your presence, knowing that with You, they can triumph over any obstacle.

In Your name, I pray. Amen.

Day 23: Promoting Healthy Conflict Resolution

Scripture: *Matthew 5:9 (KJV) - Blessed are the peacemakers: for they shall be called the children of God.*

Declaration: Today, I declare my commitment to promoting healthy conflict resolution in my child. I will teach them the art of peacemaking, emphasizing the importance of resolving conflicts peacefully and with love. I believe that in cultivating a spirit of peace, we reflect our divine heritage as children of God.

Motivation: In Matthew 5:9, Jesus blesses the peacemakers. By nurturing this quality in my child, I am empowering them to bridge divides, mend relationships, and sow seeds of

Sacred Parenting

understanding and harmony. Healthy conflict resolution fosters empathy, communication skills, and a compassionate heart, allowing us to be instruments of God's peace.

Reflection: Matthew 5:9 reminds us of the blessedness of being peacemakers. Today, I reflect on instances when peaceful resolution diffused tension and restored harmony. I contemplate the transformative power of love in conflict, understanding that it has the ability to heal wounds, nurture understanding, and strengthen relationships.

Prayer: Dear Lord, Bless my child with the spirit of a peacemaker. Guide them to resolve conflicts with love, understanding, and empathy. May they be instruments of Your peace, bringing harmony wherever there is discord. Strengthen their resolve to mend relationships and sow seeds of understanding. In their peaceful actions, may they

Sacred Parenting

reflect Your love and grace, and may they be called the children of God.

In Your name, I pray. Amen.

Day 24: Encouraging Environmental Responsibility

Scripture: *Genesis 2:15 (KJV) - And the Lord God took the man, and put him into the garden of Eden to dress it and to keep it.*

Declaration: Today, I declare my commitment to encouraging environmental responsibility in my child. I will instill in them a deep sense of respect and care for God's creation. I believe that as stewards of this Earth, it is our sacred duty to protect, preserve, and nurture the natural world that God has entrusted to us.

Motivation: In Genesis 2:15, God commands us to care for the garden He created. By teaching my child the importance of environmental responsibility, I am nurturing their awareness, empathy, and love for the Earth. Every act of conservation, no matter how small, contributes to the well-being of our planet and honors God's divine craftsmanship.

Reflection: Genesis 2:15 speaks of our responsibility to care for the garden. Today, I reflect on the beauty of nature and the role we play in its preservation. I contemplate the transformative power of mindful living, understanding that by respecting our environment, we are expressing gratitude for the abundant blessings God has bestowed upon us.

Prayer: Dear Lord, Grant my child a profound love and respect for the Earth. Help them understand the importance of environmental responsibility and inspire them to be caretakers of Your creation. May their actions reflect their gratitude for the beauty of nature, and may they be mindful stewards of the resources You have provided. Guide us as a family to make choices that honor and preserve the wonderful world You have entrusted to our care.

In Your name, I pray. Amen.

Day 25: Guiding in Healthy Eating

Scripture: *1 Corinthians 6:19-20 (KJV) - What? know ye not that your body is the temple of the Holy Ghost which is in you, which ye have of God, and ye are not your own? For ye are bought with a price: therefore, glorify God in your body, and in your spirit, which are God's.*

Declaration: Today, I declare my commitment to guiding my child in making healthy food choices. I will teach them to honor their bodies as temples of God, understanding that the food they consume profoundly impacts their physical and spiritual well-being. I believe that by nourishing our bodies with care, we glorify God's divine creation.

Motivation: In 1 Corinthians 6:19-20, we are reminded that our bodies are temples of the Holy

Ghost. By teaching my child the importance of healthy eating, I am nurturing their respect for the divine dwelling within them. Healthy food choices provide energy, vitality, and strength, allowing us to serve God and others with enthusiasm and vigor.

Reflection: 1 Corinthians 6:19-20 underscores the sacredness of our bodies. Today, I reflect on the food choices I make and their impact on my overall well-being. I contemplate the transformative power of mindful eating, understanding that it allows us to align our physical health with our spiritual connection to God.

Prayer: Dear Lord, Bless my child with wisdom and discernment in their food choices. Help them recognize the importance of nourishing their bodies as temples of the Holy Ghost. May they find joy in honoring their physical and spiritual well-being,

Sacred Parenting

Sacred Parenting

glorifying You in their actions. Guide us as a family to make choices that reflect our gratitude for the body You have given us. In Your name, I pray. Amen.

Day 26: Encouraging Lifelong Learning

Scripture: *Proverbs 1:5 (KJV) - A wise man will hear, and will increase learning; and a man of understanding shall attain unto wise counsels.*

Declaration: Today, I declare my commitment to encouraging a lifelong love for learning in my child. I will nurture their curiosity, inspire exploration, and ignite a thirst for knowledge. I believe that learning is a divine journey, enriching our minds, souls, and understanding of the world God created.

Motivation: In Proverbs 1:5, we are reminded of the value of continuous learning. By promoting a love for learning in my child, I am fostering their intellectual growth, curiosity, and creativity.

Sacred Parenting

Lifelong learning opens doors to new ideas, perspectives, and opportunities, empowering us to make informed decisions and contribute meaningfully to the world.

Reflection: Proverbs 1:5 emphasizes the importance of increasing learning. Today, I reflect on the joy of discovery and the transformative power of knowledge in my own life. I contemplate the endless possibilities that come with a curious mind, understanding that learning broadens our horizons and deepens our understanding of God's vast creation.

Prayer: Dear Lord, Bless my child with a hunger for knowledge and a love for learning. Inspire their curiosity, guide their exploration, and fill their hearts with the joy of discovery. May they approach each day with a thirst for understanding, recognizing that every piece of knowledge is a glimpse into Your divine wisdom. Grant them the resilience to face challenges in their pursuit of

Sacred Parenting

learning and the humility to acknowledge that true wisdom comes from You.

In Your name, I pray. Amen.

Day 27: Teaching Humor and Joy

Scripture: *Proverbs 17:22 (KJV) - A merry heart doeth good like a medicine: but a broken spirit drieth the bones*

Declaration: Today, I declare my commitment to nurturing humor and joy in my family. I will teach my child the healing power of laughter and a joyful spirit, understanding that a merry heart is a precious gift from God. I believe that in finding humor and joy, we uplift our spirits, strengthen our bonds, and honor the joyous life God has granted us.

Motivation: In Proverbs 17:22, we are reminded of the healing power of a merry heart. By encouraging humor and joy, I am nurturing emotional resilience, fostering positive connections, and cultivating a spirit of gratitude. Laughter lightens our burdens, deepens our relationships, and infuses our lives with warmth and happiness.

Reflection: Proverbs 17:22 speaks of the medicinal quality of a merry heart. Today, I reflect on moments of laughter and joy within my family, acknowledging the positive impact they have on our well-being. I contemplate the transformative power of humor, understanding that it bridges gaps, dispels tension, and reminds us of the abundant joy God has woven into the fabric of life.

Prayer: Dear Lord, Bless our family with laughter and joy. Grant us the ability to find humor in everyday situations and to embrace the happiness that resides in Your love. May our home be filled with laughter that heals, joy that uplifts, and love that binds us together. Teach my child the value of

Sacred Parenting

a merry heart, and may they carry the gift of joy into the world, sharing Your love through their laughter.

In Your name, I pray.

Amen.

Day 28: Promoting Resourcefulness

Scripture: *Philippians 4:13 (KJV) - I can do all things through Christ which strengtheneth me.*

Declaration: Today, I declare my commitment to promoting resourcefulness in my child. I will inspire them to find solutions, utilize their talents, and manage their resources effectively, understanding that with Christ's strength, all challenges can be overcome. I believe that resourcefulness is a divine gift, empowering us to adapt, grow, and thrive in any circumstance.

Motivation: In Philippians 4:13, we are reminded of our strength through Christ. By promoting resourcefulness, I am nurturing my child's creativity, problem-solving skills, and resilience. Resourceful individuals find opportunities where others see obstacles, and they utilize their talents and resources effectively to create positive change. With Christ's guidance, they can overcome any challenge.

Reflection: Philippians 4:13 speaks of the strength we find through Christ. Today, I reflect on moments when resourcefulness led to solutions and growth. I contemplate the transformative power of creativity and adaptability, understanding that with God's strength, we can navigate any situation. I acknowledge the talents and resources within our family, grateful for the opportunities they provide.

Prayer: Dear Lord, Bless my child with the gift of resourcefulness. Guide them to find creative solutions, utilize their talents, and manage their resources effectively. May they approach challenges with confidence, knowing that with Your strength, all things are possible. Grant them wisdom to see opportunities in every obstacle and

Sacred Parenting

courage to pursue innovative solutions. In their resourcefulness, may they glorify Your name and inspire others.

In Your powerful and guiding name, I pray. Amen.

Day 29: Cultivating Mindfulness

Scripture: *Philippians 4:8 (KJV) - Finally, brethren, whatsoever things are true, whatsoever things are honest, whatsoever things are just, whatsoever things are pure, whatsoever things are lovely, whatsoever things are of good report; if there be any virtue, and if there be any praise, think on these things.*

Declaration: Today, I declare my dedication to cultivating mindfulness in my child. I will teach them the importance of positive thinking and focusing on virtuous and uplifting thoughts, as encouraged by Philippians 4:8. I believe that in nurturing a mindful spirit, we invite peace, joy, and divine wisdom into our lives.

Sacred Parenting

Motivation: In Philippians 4:8, we are guided to think on things that are true, honest, just, pure, lovely, and of good report. By cultivating mindfulness, I am empowering my child to filter their thoughts, choosing positivity over negativity, gratitude over complaint, and love over fear. A mindful spirit opens the door to a world of possibilities, fostering inner peace and resilience.

Reflection: Philippians 4:8 directs our focus toward virtuous thoughts. Today, I reflect on the impact of positive thinking in my own life, acknowledging the transformative power it holds. I contemplate the peace that comes with a mindful spirit, understanding that it aligns us with God's truth and love. I embrace the joy found in uplifting thoughts, recognizing them as pathways to spiritual enlightenment.

Prayer: Dear Lord,

Grant my child the gift of mindfulness. Guide them to think on things that are true, honest, just,

Sacred Parenting

pure, lovely, and of good report. May their thoughts be reflections of Your divine wisdom and love. Help them choose positivity, gratitude, and kindness in every situation. In their mindfulness, may they find peace, joy, and a deeper connection with You. Bless their hearts with uplifting thoughts, and may they shine as beacons of Your light in the world.

In Your name, I pray.

Amen.

Day 30: Reflecting on God's Plan

Scripture: *Jeremiah 29:11 (KJV) - For I know the thoughts that I think toward you, saith the Lord, thoughts of peace, and not of evil, to give you an expected end.*

Declaration: Today, I declare my trust in God's plan for my child. I will reflect on His divine guidance, knowing that He holds thoughts of peace, hope, and purpose for each child. I believe that God's plan is filled with blessings and a future brimming with hope, and I trust in His perfect design for my child's life.

Motivation: In Jeremiah 29:11, God assures us of His benevolent thoughts and a future filled with hope. As parents, trusting in His divine plan provides us with comfort and reassurance. By reflecting on God's guidance, we find strength to face uncertainties, knowing that His purpose unfolds in perfect timing and that His blessings are beyond measure.

Reflection: Jeremiah 29:11 speaks of God's peaceful thoughts and hopeful plans. Today, I reflect on moments when I witnessed God's guidance in my child's life. I contemplate the beauty of His unfolding plan, understanding that His wisdom surpasses our understanding. I find solace in His promise, embracing the peace that comes from trusting in His divine purpose.

Prayer: Dear Lord,

I entrust my child into Your loving hands, acknowledging Your divine plan for their life. Thank You for the peace and hope Your promise brings. Help me trust in Your guidance and surrender to Your perfect will. May my child always walk in the light of Your purpose, finding hope in every step they take. Bless them

Sacred Parenting

abundantly, Lord, and guide them toward a future filled with Your love, grace, and blessings.

In Your name, I pray. Amen.

Conclusion

In this 30-day devotional journey, we have explored the essential aspects of parenting through the lens of faith, guided by the timeless wisdom of the Scriptures. As parents, we are entrusted with the sacred duty of nurturing, guiding, and loving our children, and in doing so, we are called to reflect the qualities of God's love in our everyday lives.

Through prayer, reflection, and dedication, we have delved into the fundamental principles of parenting: love, patience, kindness, respect, gratitude, discipline, forgiveness, confidence, responsibility, humility, empathy, trust, perseverance, healthy relationships, decision-making, contentment, teamwork, creativity, self-reflection, servanthood, time management, and mindfulness. By grounding our parenting in these

Sacred Parenting

principles, we create a nurturing environment where our children can flourish and grow in the light of God's love.

We have been reminded of the divine assurance found in Scripture, such as Philippians 4:13, "I can do all things through Christ which strengtheneth me," and Jeremiah 29:11, "For I know the thoughts that I think toward you, saith the Lord, thoughts of peace, and not of evil, to give you an expected end." These verses reinforce our trust in God's strength and His unwavering plan for our lives and the lives of our children.

As we conclude this devotional, let us carry these teachings in our hearts, allowing them to shape our parenting journey. Let us continue to seek God's guidance, trusting in His divine wisdom, and nurturing our children with love, faith, and unwavering dedication. May our homes be filled with the grace of God, and may our children grow

Sacred Parenting

up knowing the depth of His love through our actions, words, and the values we instill in them.

May God bless our families abundantly, guiding us on this sacred journey of parenthood, and may His love continue to illuminate our paths now and always.

In His love and grace,

Made in the USA
Columbia, SC
29 June 2024

37d2a40f-02ab-417b-aa12-d9a9cd89b7f7R02